First Steps in Science

Teacher's Resource Book

First Steps in Science

Teacher's
Resource Book

Carrie Branigan

Text © Carrie Branigan 2003
Original illustrations © Nelson Thornes Ltd 2003

Published in 2003 by:
Nelson Thornes Ltd
Delta Place
27 Bath Road
CHELTENHAM
GL53 7TH
United Kingdom

03 04 05 06/ 10 9 8 7 6 5 4 3 2 1

A catalogue record for this book is available from the British
Library

ISBN 0 7487 6864 5

Design and page make-up by Lorraine Inglis

Printed and bound in Great Britain by
Ashford Colour Press

Contents

Introduction

The purpose of writing science materials for teachers in the reception class is to show that science can be seen as a natural and stimulating starting point for planning other 'areas of learning'. What the materials provide is a co-ordinated approach to teaching, starting from children's own experiences and crucially using play, i.e. exploratory, role play and games, as a vehicle for learning.

The materials are cross referenced to the 'stepping stones' and 'early learning goals' to ensure that there is continuity and progression in children's learning. The materials, therefore, provide a smooth transition to the National Curriculum.

What the materials contain

Overview of units

This is an explanation of how the First Steps in Science resources tie in with the curriculum guidance for the foundation stage – the links between the class activities, 'stepping stones', 'early learning goals', planned play opportunities and the relevant Big Story Book text (see pages 8 and 9).

Unit guidance and activity plans: six units (1 per half term)

Each unit includes a single page 'Unit Guidance' plus a complete set of six tried and tested practical activities (1 per page). Each plan includes references to resources, safety, links to other areas of learning, assessment criteria and role play opportunities. The use of role play and other play opportunities, based on the unit theme, are either integrated into the main activity or used as an additional activity. (see page 10 for a description of the content of a lesson plan).

Big Story Book: six stories (1 per unit).

Image Bank: 96 picture cards (16 per unit).

The materials provide a framework for developing children's literacy skills by using story texts and pictures as an essential part of each unit. In addition, children's numeracy and information and communication technology skills are a coherent feature within the planned activities.

First Steps in Science provides a complete guide for planning children's learning in science in the reception class and a co-ordinated starting point for other areas of learning.

An Overview of Units for Year R

Each unit, such as 'At Home', is planned to address the broad aims of the foundation stage curriculum through these specific areas of science, stories from the Big Story Book and supplementary role play.

Unit	Areas in science	Role Play	Big Story Book
All About Me	Recognition of body parts and feeling unwell	House Hospital Doctor's surgery Baby clinic	On the way to the park
Day and Night	Exploration of light sources and shadows	House Cave Shadow theatre	Can you see my car?
At Home	Exploration of everyday materials inside the house	House Three Bears' House Café	What shall I wear today?
Moving Around	Exploration of movement of themselves, toys and other objects	House Garage Toy shop/factory	A plasticine snowman
Growing Up	Recognition of changes from babies to adults and how to take care of one another	House Vet's practice	My shoes
Outdoors	Recognition of living things, their features and habitats	Garden centre	Down by the shed

Unit Guidance

Image Bank

Big Story Book

Activity Plans

6 5 4 3 2 1

Foundation stage curriculum

Each Unit Guidance page indicates how the unit contributes towards the six areas of learning within the foundation stage curriculum: personal, social and emotional development (PS&E); communication, language and literacy (CL&L); mathematical development (MD); knowledge and understanding of the world (K&U); physical development (PD); and creative development (CD).

The activities in **First Steps in Science** are designed to tally with the curriculum guidance as set out for the foundation stage – i.e. the early learning goals and corresponding 'stepping stones'.

Examples of identifiable early learning goals generally addressed by the **First Steps in Science** lessons are:
- Continue to be interested, excited and motivated to learn (PS&E)

- Be confident to try new activities, initiate ideas and speak in a familiar group (PS&E)

- Extend their vocabulary, exploring the meanings and sounds of new words (CL&L)

- Look closely at similarities, differences, patterns and change (K&U)

- Handle tools, objects, construction and malleable materials safely and with increasing control (K&U)

- Use imagination in art and design, music, dance, imaginative and role play and stories (CD)

Other early learning goals are more specifically relevant to individual units, though not exclusively so, for example:

Day and Night: Use talk to organise sequence and clarify thinking, ideas, feelings and events (CL&L)

At Home: Investigate objects and materials by using all of their senses as appropriate (K&U)

Moving Around: Ask questions about why things happen and how things work (K&U)

Growing Up: Find out about past and present events in their own lives, and in those of their families and other people they know (K&U)

Outdoors: Find out about, and identify, some features of living things, objects and events they observe (K&U)

5–14 Guidelines for Environmental Studies — Science

First Steps in Science provides a firm foundation in knowledge, understanding and skills for children who are working towards Level A in Science. A wide variety of activities spring from the familiar starting point of children's everyday experiences, including role play, using and reinforcing a range of cross-curricular skills. There are close links right across the curriculum, especially with language work, and the whole approach is set firmly in the context of 'developing informed attitudes'.

A description of the content of an activity plan (6 per unit)

Activity number: Key question

Purpose of activity

Introducing, continuing or extending learning

Vocabulary

Focused on the particular activity

Assessment

Children will be able to:
- *Refer to relevant stepping stones and early learning goals and/or other skills gained through the activity*

Whole class or group activity

The text in this section provides an approach to answering the 'key question'. It describes the structure and content of an activity with enough detail to give the practitioner a useful 'picture' of the session, e.g. teaching strategies and classroom organisation. The activity also shows how it relates to previous or forthcoming sessions.

The relevant story from the Big Story Book and the individual photos or illustrations from the Image Bank are identified and their use explained as an essential part of the activity.

Other related activities:

A description of activities that relate to the 'key question' across other areas of learning or as an extension of the science activity.

Resources and preparation

Outlines type of preparation, e.g. reference to Big Story Book and Image Bank cards and materials and equipment required for the activity

 Highlights safety considerations where necessary

Role play

A unit-related description of a planned role play situation integrated into the activity or as an additional feature

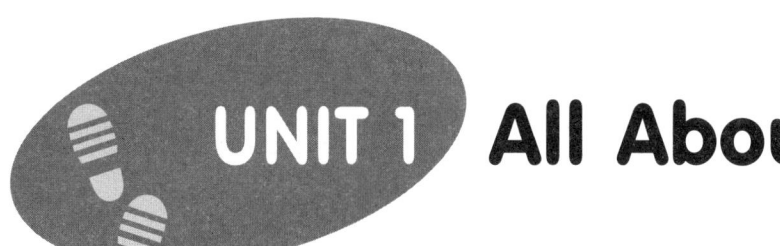

UNIT 1 All About Me

Unit guidance

Purpose of unit:

- To look at body parts, how they move and what they can do

- To recognise what happens when you are ill

By the end of the topic children will be able to:
- Find out more about themselves

- Identify features about themselves

- Look at similarities and differences about themselves

Teaching resources

Big Story Book: 'On the way to the park'

Image Bank

Display and collections: Shiny objects

Children's artwork, e.g. playtime pictures

Role play

House

Doctor's surgery

Baby clinic

Hospital

Activities

1 What do I look like?
Exploring and talking about mirrors

2 What are my body parts?
Recognising and naming body parts

3 Just like me?
Recognising similarities and differences

4 How can I move?
Exploring movement using legs and feet

5 What can I do?
Recognising use of hands and fingers

6 What happens when I am ill?
Recognising illness and looking after ourselves

Links to other areas of learning:

PS&E: express needs and feelings; self-image; co-operation

CL&L: speak about wants and interests; talk about events; look for and retrieve information from books; attempt writing for different purposes

MD: show awareness of symmetry; use language such as 'longer'; grouping objects

K&U: construct objects for a purpose

PD: move in different ways; move confidently and with imagination

CD: make constructions, collage, drawings and dances

Activity 1 What do I look like?

Purpose of activity

To introduce mirrors and observe reflections

Vocabulary

me, face, nose, eyes, hair, mouth, mirror, reflection

Assessment

Children will be able to:

● Explore mirrors and their reflection

● Talk about their reflections in simple ways, e.g. 'me', 'I can see me', 'I can see my nose and eyes', 'I can't see myself very well in this one'

Whole class or group activity

Show children Image Bank pictures 1.1 and 1.2 and talk about what the pictures show. Using a large mirror, show the children how they are reflected in the mirror. Use the mirror to look at your own reflection and talk about what you see, e.g. 'I've got brown eyes and a smiley mouth.' Use the range of listed vocabulary.

Give out a flat mirror to each child and ask them to look at themselves and see if they can see different parts of their face. Encourage exploration and talk about their reflections. Provide paper and pencils to encourage drawings.

Look together at the collection of shiny objects (enough for more than one each) and encourage talk and simple description of the reflections in different objects. Encourage children to draw their reflections seen in a variety of shiny objects.

End of activity (or later in day): talk about how well they saw themselves in the mirrors/shiny objects. Display drawings with the class collection of shiny objects.

Other related activities

Exploration: investigate the variety of shiny objects and mirrors in displayed collection; encourage pupils to mimic different facial expressions in mirrors

Art: painting own face or friend's face

Writing/drawing: continue reflections in stories and pictures

Physical: copy friend's movement like a mirror

Resources and preparation

Image Bank pictures 1.1 and 1.2; various shiny objects (flat plastic and small glass); flat mirrors; paper and coloured pencils

 Ensure that masking tape is stuck around the edges of any glass mirrors

Role play

House containing domestic play equipment, including mirrors and drawing materials

Activity ❷ What are my body parts?

Purpose of activity

To introduce the main external parts of the body

Vocabulary

body, head, shoulders, knees, toes, eyes, ears, foot, feet, etc.

Assessment

Children will be able to:

● Recognise, name and point to body parts

Resources and preparation

Image Bank pictures 1.3 and 1.4; large sheets of paper joined for body drawing/display; card labels of body parts for the body display

Role play

House containing domestic play equipment

Whole class or group activity

Begin the session by singing and pointing to the parts of the body in the song 'Head, shoulders, knees and toes'. Ensure all children are joining in and help them point to the parts if necessary. Show children Image Bank picture 1.3 and demonstrate how the picture follows the song. Show the next picture (1.4) and sing the song with the new body parts; practise before singing and pointing.

Ask children to make up their own version of the song, as individuals or in pairs, and then sing it to teach the rest of the class or group their own song.

Draw around a child or adult, naming the parts as they are drawn round. With the drawn body on the floor, sing the two versions of the song again, pointing to the parts on the drawing. Finish by giving children the chance to place a card label on the body display before it is put on the wall.

Later in day (or next day): change the labels on the display to see if it is noticed. Review the body parts and rearrange labels with the children.

The body display could also show x-rays to be used later for the hospital role play.

Other related activities:

Language: cut out labels and stick them onto a body to replicate the class display

Relevant puzzles/games/fiction and non-fiction books: depicting body parts for further paired or group speaking and listening

Plasticine/playdough: making body shapes

Cooking: read *The Gingerbread Man* story and make gingerbread people *(see page 58 for recipe)*

Activity ③ Just like me?

Purpose of activity

To group similarities and differences in hair colour

Vocabulary

hair, hair colour (black, brown, mousy, blond, red, grey, etc.)

Assessment

Children will be able to:

● Examine their hair colour to find out more about each other

● Find out about and identify hair colour of themselves and their friends, looking closely at similarities and differences

Whole class or group activity

Introduce session by asking questions about body parts: 'How many arms do we all have?' 'How many eyes, how many elbows?' etc. 'Does that mean we are all the same?' Talk about the differences with the children and use their observations to structure the conversation.

Summarise the discussion by showing the Image Bank pictures 1.5 and 1.6. Ask 'How am I the same as my friends?' Talk about children in the photos and continue session by lining up children and asking them to follow your instructions: 'If you have brown hair, stand here. If you have black hair, stand here.' Help organise children and sit them down to count each group. Ask, 'Which group has the most children with the same colour hair? Which group has the fewest?' Give each child a sticky label to colour in, or a piece of coloured sticky paper, to use to plot the class/group graph. Bring children together around the empty block graph and ask each child, in turn, to stick on their label. Discuss the graph as it is being constructed. Count each column and match the number to the original groups. Ask, 'Where will I go?' 'Where will ... go?' Help them look at your hair colour and stick on your own label. Ask questions again about the number of people in each column.

Later in the day (or next day): compare the graph with another class or group to show how there are similarities and differences between lots of children. Display graphs.

Other related activities:

Mathematics: group dolls, puppets or small world characters in different ways related to body parts or hair colour

ICT: use the results of an eye colour survey to construct a graph

Resources and preparation

Image Bank pictures 1.5 and 1.6; large class block graph (hair colour and numbers as axes); sticky labels; one for each child; brown, black, yellow and orange crayons, or coloured sticky paper similar to hair colours in class; Image Bank pictures 1.13–1.16 (for role play)

Role play

Begin hospital, include x-rays, mirrors, charts, etc., to illustrate body parts

Activity ④ How can I move?

Purpose of activity

To recognise how their bodies move using their legs and feet

Vocabulary

leg, legs, foot, feet, toe, toes, jump, jumping, hop, hopping, walk, walking, run, etc.

Assessment

Children will be able to:

- Show an awareness of how their legs and feet can be made to jump, hop, etc.

- Look closely at similarities and differences about how their bodies are moving

Resources and preparation

Image Bank pictures 1.7 and 1.8; Big Story Book story 'On the way to the park'; Flipchart/board; A5 card (optional); Image Bank pictures 1.13–1.16 (for role play)

⚠ Make sure you have enough space for movement (classroom/hall/outdoors)

Whole class or group activity

Refer to the large body display and check the children's knowledge of the labels. Focus on legs and feet and show Image Bank pictures 1.7 and 1.8 to stimulate discussion about which body parts are being used to make movements.

Continue by asking children to follow instructions as a 'Simon says' type activity, for example: 'Simon says jump, hop, skip', etc. Extend the activity by developing a simple sequence, for example: 'Simon says: do a jump, a twist and a hop.' Ensure all the children can be supported to follow instructions.

Show children how to think of a sequence of movements and draw it as pin-people on A5 pieces of card. Give out cards to pairs of children as guides to drawing their own sequences. Alternatively draw a sequence on a flipchart or board and ask for other suggestions for sequences. Continue by putting a number of sequences together for performance. Monitor children's performances and talk to them about how their legs and feet are being used.

Collect words from the group to be added as labels to the body display. Talk about how their legs moved when jumping. Was it different or the same as when they were hopping, etc?

Read 'On the way to the park' from the Big Story Book and use it to stimulate more words and movements.

Role play/small world

Hospital, include x-rays, charts, etc., to illustrate body parts. Role play child or doll having an accident in the park

Other related activities:

Physical: continue focusing on movement of different parts of the body and extend to 'over', 'under' type vocabulary

Small play/puppets: act out story of journey to the park from the Big Story Book

Drawing and writing: make pictures and descriptions of playtimes, with children moving around, skipping, etc.

Activity ⑤ What can I do?

Purpose of activity

To recognise how their hands and fingers are useful for many everyday tasks

Vocabulary:

hand, hands, finger, fingers, thumb, thumbs, and related simple descriptive activity words such as: threading, squashing, rolling

Assessment

Children will be able to:

● Examine their use of hands/fingers to find out what they can do

● Describe what their hands and fingers can do, for example: 'my thumb and big finger make the thread go through the beads'

Whole class or group activities

Introduce the session with familiar action songs using fingers to begin to develop the theme of how we use hands and fingers. Show and talk about the Image Bank pictures 1.9 and 1.10 to extend to other actions/activities.

Show sets of activities and demonstrate how to focus their work on the use of hands and fingers, for example: manipulating playdough and asking questions such as, 'What can my hands and fingers do with the dough?' Discuss responses: squashing, rolling, flattening dough, etc. Ensure simple descriptive vocabulary is used. Show other activities available and remind them of what they are going to be doing and talking about.

Organise groups to use various materials in a circus of activities and ensure the children focus on how they can use their hands and fingers. Encourage the use of appropriate vocabulary.

At the end of the session talk about what the children have done and how they have used their hands and fingers. Collect simple descriptive words to add to labels for the body display, e.g.: flicking, holding, rolling, feeling.

Review the body display and talk about the areas covered during the unit.

Other related activities:

Drawing and writing: label a drawing of themselves making a plasticine model

Physical: talk about and explore use of hands and fingers using small apparatus

---

Resources and preparation

Image Bank pictures 1.9 and 1.10; playdough *(recipe on p.58)*/ plasticine/clay/wet sand, etc.; beads and thread; finger paints, pencils, crayons; construction materials, including reclaimed materials

Image Bank pictures 1.13–1.16 (for role play)

Role play/small world

Hospital: start to include a baby clinic and/or a chemist

Activity 6 What happens when I am ill?

Purpose of activity

To introduce the symptoms and care needed when we are ill

Vocabulary

ill, sick, not well, hot, cold, fever, temperature, thermometer, thirsty, not hungry, spots, itchy, look after, sleep, medicine, tablets, syrup, etc.

Assessment

Children will be able to:
- Show an awareness of being ill and related symptoms and care
- Talk about being ill and ask questions about illness and care

Whole class or group activity

Use a doll from the baby clinic to stimulate a discussion about feeling ill. Refer to the doll as a focus for discussion by describing the doll's symptoms, for example: crying and hot. Open the discussion to their own experiences; talk about being ill at home or going to the doctor. 'What happens when *you* feel ill? How do you get looked after?'

Use the Image Bank pictures 1.11 and 1.12 with real objects to clarify what help may be needed, e.g.: hot water bottle, thermometer. Summarise the discussion by asking what would help the doll from your initial discussion. Give the doll to a small group of children to continue the play in the role play area.

Organise the other groups for related activities, e.g. small world hospital play, puppets, writing/drawing about feeling ill, reading books and exploring strip thermometers.

You could set up a separate domestic house play area and perhaps encourage a visit from a child dressed as a doctor. You could also set up a table as a chemist and ask children what the chemist would need, e.g. equipment, posters. Monitor the work of groups and focus any discussions on the symptoms of illness and looking after somebody. Move groups around or allow them to choose different activities.

Bring the groups together to discuss the activities they have been doing and show any drawing or writing plus any 'drama' activities that children may want to act out with the puppets.

Other related activities:

Drawing/writing: make a class book about being ill or about their own visits to the doctor or hospital

ICT: construct a class graph about the different illnesses in the class — some children could use a tally chart to collect information

Resources and preparation

Image Bank pictures 1.11 and 1.12; role play hospital equipment, e.g. doll, thermometer, stethoscope; small world hospital and puppet; Image Bank pictures 1.13–1.16 (for role play)

⚠ Remind children never to touch or take medicine without an adult present

Role play/small world

Hospital

UNIT 2 Day and Night

Unit guidance

Purpose of unit:

- To explore and talk about light sources, shadows and darkness

By the end of the topic children will be able to:
- Talk about what is seen and what is happening
- Examine objects and comment on patterns
- Examine objects and find out more about them

Activities

1 Where does light come from?
   Observing and recognising light sources

2 How can we see in the dark?
   Exploring the use of torches

3 How can we be seen in the dark?
   Testing and using reflectors

4 How can we make shadows?
   Making and exploring shadows

5 What can our shadows do?
   Exploring shadows

6 How can shadows be used?
   Using a shadow theatre

Links to other areas of learning:

PS&E: using increasing confidence, initiative and working with each other

CL&L: increasing confidence in communicating through speech, story and writing

MD: making and recognising shapes

K&U: constructing shadow puppets

PD: using equipment and tools

CD: exploring and recreating light and shadows

Teaching resources

Big Story Book: 'Can you see my car?'

Image Bank

Display and collections: light sources

Children's artwork: shiny collages

Role play

House

Cave

Shadow theatre

Activity ❶ Where does light come from?

Purpose of activity

To introduce children to the idea and use of light sources

Vocabulary

light, dark, bright, brighter, see, not see, names of light sources

Assessment

Children will be able to:

● Show curiosity and talk about what can be seen

● Examine where light is coming from

● Look closely at similarities and differences about light sources

Whole class or group activity

Look around the classroom to see where light comes from, e.g. the sun, strip lights, computer screen. Talk about and point to how bright the lights are.

Use the Image Bank pictures of a living room in daylight and at night time with lights on and off. Discuss where the light comes from in the pictures, e.g. window, TV, lamps, etc.

Remind children of the Image Bank pictures, ask children to draw a picture of their bedroom or other room at home and show, with a yellow crayon, where the light comes from in their room. Alternatively, using a selection of pictures from the Image Bank, ask children to talk about the lights in the variety of scenes. Have drawing materials available.

Finish the session by showing children's drawings and photos talking about the different light sources within the rooms.

Other related activities:

Exploration: explore a variety of light sources on display, talking about how the light is turned on and off and how bright it is

Knowledge/understanding: discuss other uses of light, e.g. candles in religious festivals

Creative: cut and stick pictures of rooms and lights

Resources and preparation

Image Bank pictures 2.1–2.5; drawing paper; pencils and yellow coloured pencils; light sources: computer screen, torches, lamps, candles, main lights, etc.

Role play

House containing domestic play equipment, including battery operated lights: torches/lamps and drawing materials

Activity ❷ How can we see in the dark?

Purpose of activity

To introduce the idea that darkness is the absence of light and that torches can be used to see in the dark

Vocabulary

dark, light, darker, darkness, no light, torch, torches, bright, brighter

Assessment

Children will be able to:

- Talk about what can be seen or what is happening

- Show an awareness of changes in light and dark

- Begin to ask questions about what is happening

Whole class or group activity

Begin session in a room that can be darkened as much as possible. Show children an object or a picture that they are going to try to see as the room gets darker. Gradually turn the lights down, then off, or cover windows. As the room is getting darker, ask children what they can see and whether they can still see the object or picture.

Begin to turn up the lights or uncover windows and gradually bring light back into the room, asking the same questions about what they can see. Repeat the exercise or parts of it if necessary to make sure all children realise the differences between lightness and darkness.

Show children the Image Bank pictures 2.6–2.9 so that they can talk about seeing in the dark. Show how the set of torches works and give one out to each child so that they can explore the torch light in the room when light and in the dark. Direct them to using the torch on the ceiling, walls and floors — not under things yet!

Once the children have explored the room with torches read the story 'Can you see my car?' using torches to support the text. Once the story has been read, darken the room once more and ask children to find objects hidden under cupboards and trolleys as in the story. Finish by reading the story once more.

Talk about the recent collection of shiny objects made when they were looking at their reflections. Make collection again.

Other related activities:

Exploration: torches in 'cave'

Story: 'Going on a bear hunt' — the above activity can be repeated this time using small teddy bears to be found in the darkened room or cave

Resources and preparation

Image Bank pictures 2.6–2.9; Big Story Book story 'Can you see my car?'; torches (enough for one each); 'cave' (table/corner of room covered in fabric); objects to be hidden in room; Image Bank pictures 2.10 and 2.11 (for role play)

 Ensure that children are warned about the room becoming dark and that they do not look directly at bright light sources

Role play

Cave with torches and hidden objects to be found

Activity ❸ How can we be seen in the dark?

Purpose of activity

To introduce and test ideas about using reflectors that can be seen in the dark

Vocabulary

light, dark, night, no light, reflector, see, not see

Assessment

Children will be able to:

● Talk about what is seen

● Show an awareness of how reflectors work

● Explore and find out more about a variety of reflectors

Whole class or group activity

Show children Image Bank pictures 2.12 and 2.13. Talk about how the children are wearing reflectors to make sure they can be seen in the dark and how children without reflectors are not seen so clearly. Using 'people' templates ask children to dress the 'people' in coats and hats, using a variety of materials, as if they were going out for a walk in the dark. Children will be aware about the need to use reflectors but the activity needs to show children why, and how difficult it can be to see dark clothes in the dark.

Using the darkened room or the classroom 'cave' ask children to test whether the people templates can be seen very easily using their torches.

Show children a dressed template already prepared with shiny or reflective material on the 'coat'. Demonstrate how this person can be more easily seen compared with one of theirs. To help in the comparison further, show the photo of the 'at night' street scene again (2.12 and 2.13) where children are walking with and without reflectors.

With other people templates and a selection of fabrics and shiny materials or reflectors, ask children to dress the people again to make sure they can be seen in the dark. Test their people in the darkened room or cave alongside their original templates.

Other related activities:

Art: making a collage of shiny paper

Resources and preparation

Image Bank pictures 2.12 and 2.13; 'people' templates, enough for 2 or 3 per child; torches; dark fabrics and shiny fabrics and materials; glue and scissors; Image Bank pictures 2.10 and 2.11 (for role play)

⚠ Ensure children recognise road safety issues

Role play

Cave with torches and hidden objects to be found, including reflectors

Activity ❹ How can we make shadows?

Purpose of activity

To introduce children to making and recognising shadows of objects

Vocabulary

light, dark, shadow, names of objects

Assessment

Children will be able to:

● Talk about what is seen

● Show an awareness of how shadows are made

● Explore and find out more about shadows

Whole class or group activity

Using an OHP, show children how shadows can be made with objects and hands on a wall. Talk about where the light is coming from and how the shadow is made. Use a variety of objects and the Image Bank picture 2.14 to demonstrate shadows. See if the children can work out what shadows are from their shapes, e.g. teddy bear.

Show children that shadows can be made by other lights and that some are not so good at casting shadows, such as candles. Give each child a torch and ask them to use it around the room to make shadows of objects. Give children a few minutes to explore the best shadows they can find and then ask them to show everyone else.

Ask them to work with a friend to draw their shadows — one holding the torch, the other drawing the shadow on white paper taped against a wall.

Finish the session by showing examples of the drawn shadows to see if the shape can be recognised.

Other related activities:

Exploration: continue making shadows and shapes

Art: drawing and cutting out shapes of shadows

Resources and preparation

Image Bank picture 2.14; OHP and screen; white paper stuck to walls; torches (one each); candles; Image Bank pictures 2.10 and 2.11 (for role play)

 Ensure that children are aware that they ought not to look directly at bright lights and they must never play with an exposed flame

Role play

Cave with torches and hidden objects to be found, including reflectors

Activity ⑤ What can our shadows do?

Purpose of activity

To explore and observe children's own shadows

Vocabulary

shadow, dark, move, moving, shape

Assessment

Children will be able to:

● Talk about what is seen

● Show an awareness of what shadows can do

● Explore and find out more about shadows

Whole class or group activity

Using the Image Bank pictures 2.15 and 2.16 review how shadows are made, their shapes and how children can make shadows outside. Take the children outside to explore their shadows. Talk to them about the shape and size of their shadows and how the shadow moves in exactly the same way as they do. Ask children to jump, run and make different shapes with their bodies and to notice what their shadows do.

   Ask them to make shapes together in pairs, or to try to step on each other's shadows.

   As a class or group, act out songs or nursery rhymes with actions, e.g. 'In and out the dusty bluebells', and focus children's attention on what their shadows are doing.

   Finish with a 'crocodile' of children walking around the playground, playing 'follow my leader' and watching how their shadows change at the same time.

Other related activities:

Exploration: continue shadow exploration outside and draw round the shadows with chalk to show different actions and shapes

Art: cut and stick shadow pictures using black and white paper

Dance: create shadow dances in the playground with or without music

Resources and preparation

Image Bank pictures 2.15 and 2.16; a clear sunny day!

⚠ Make sure children know never to look directly at the sun

Role play

Begin the shadow theatre so that children can begin to tell stories using shadows

Activity 6 How can shadows be used?

Purpose of activity

To use the idea of shadows in a more creative context

Vocabulary

light, dark, shadow, puppet, see, not see

Assessment

Children will be able to:
- Talk about what is seen
- Show an awareness of what shadows can do
- Explore and find out more about shadows

Resources and preparation

Image Bank picture 2.16; materials for shadow puppets, e.g. card, sticks, fabric, sellotape; OHP; translucent screen; Image Bank pictures 2.15 and 2.16 (for role play)

 Ensure that children do not look directly at bright lights

Role play

Shadow theatre

Whole class or group activity

Show children the Image Bank picture 2.16 of the puppet theatre and show the class how shadow theatre works using the shadows from hands, fingers or puppets made from card on sticks. Ask a couple of children to try the theatre with puppets so that others can see. Allow all pupils to have a go so that they can see how the puppets need to be placed in front of the light. Talk about how their shadow puppets work, reviewing the previous work on shadows.

Once children recognise how the theatre works ask them to work in pairs and choose a nursery rhyme or a story. Once they have decided on their idea, ask them to make puppets of the characters from their story out of card and sticks.

Talk about what is important when making a shadow puppet. Make sure the children understand that the outline has to define their chosen character, e.g. a rounded body for Humpty Dumpty, or curly-toed shoes for the Genie of the Lamp.

Each pair can then perform their story in the shadow theatre.

Other related activities:

Exploration: shadow puppets using torches against a wall

Art: make other puppet characters

Construction: make jointed puppets using split pins on arm and leg joints

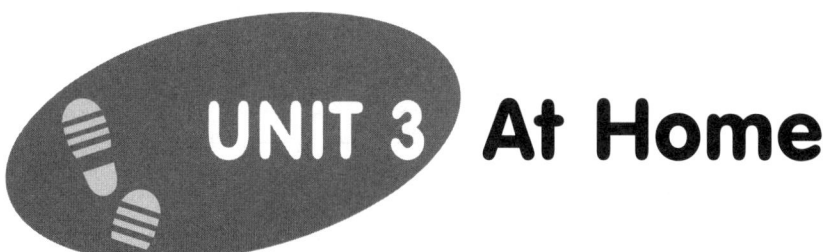

UNIT 3 At Home

Unit guidance

Purpose of unit:

To explore materials inside the house, including fabrics, objects and food

By the end of the topic children will be able to:
- Show curiosity, observe and manipulate objects
- Describe simple features
- Examine objects, notice and comment on patterns
- Investigate objects and materials by using all of their senses
- Examine objects and find out more about them

Activities

1 What shall I wear today?
   Exploring waterproof materials

2 Which fabric is the best?
   Testing fabrics for their suitability

3 What is it made of?
   Exploring everyday materials

4 Which porridge tastes the best?
   Making and tasting flavoured porridge

5 What do I like best?
   Tasting food types

6 Which things work by electricity?
   Recognising how electricity can be used

Links to other areas of learning:

PS&E: show confidence, initiative, involvement, motivation and interest

CL&L: recognise familiar stories and characters, discuss and extend vocabulary

MD: match sizes and shapes, use related language, e.g. bigger

K&U: construct models and use ICT to communicate

CD: make paintings, cutting and sticking collages and drawings

PD: use and handle tools for construction

Teaching resources

Big Story Book: 'What shall I wear today?'

Image Bank

Display and collections: fabrics and everyday objects

Children's artwork: story character's cottage

Role play

House

Goldilocks story

Café

Activity **1** What shall I wear today?

Purpose of activity

To introduce and test the uses of waterproof fabrics and materials

Vocabulary

water, wet, drip, dripping, drop, droplet, waterproof; clothing names: e.g. wellies; names of fabrics: e.g. plastic, rubber

Assessment

Children will be able to:

- Recognise clothing as waterproof

- Examine clothing to find out more about them

- Describe features of waterproof clothing, e.g. plastic, shiny

Whole class or group activity

Using the story 'What shall I wear today?' dress up a child as the story progresses. Use the story from the Big Story Book, Image Bank picture 3.1 and acting to ask why all of the different types of clothes were needed. Talk about warmth, protection and waterproofing using examples from their own experiences, such as playtimes or looking after a baby brother or sister.

Focus the children's attention on waterproof clothes showing Image Bank picture 3.2. Squirt a few drops of water on a pair of wellies. Watch together to see what happens to the water on the surface of the wellies. Talk about the water droplets and encourage the vocabulary of 'dripping down', 'falling', etc. Show children the collection of waterproof objects such as umbrellas, macs and wellies and show them how to use a pipette to check how waterproof the objects are. Ask children to test the variety of objects with pipettes and ask them to look at how the water drips off each object. One group, outside, could test waterproof clothing worn by an adult.

After exploring the objects talk about their findings together and ask some children to show others what they have found out.

Other related activities:

Exploration: continue with other waterproof and non-waterproof clothing; use watering cans to simulate drips and drops like rain outdoors or in a water tray

ICT: make rainy day pictures using an art program

Art: cut and stick rainy day pictures

Discussion: talk about the clothing in Image Bank picture 3.3

Resources and preparation

Image Bank pictures 3.1–3.3; Big Story Book story 'What shall I wear today?'; old newspapers; child's outdoor clothing; a collection of waterproof clothing including wellies; pipettes (one each); small pots of water

Role play/small world

House containing domestic play equipment, including outdoor clothing

Activity **2** Which fabric is the best?

Purpose of activity

To test a variety of fabrics and select one for a particular purpose related to a story character

Vocabulary

descriptions of fabric: e.g. stretchy, spongy, squashy, sparkly, shiny, waterproof

Assessment

Children will be able to:

- Sort the fabrics suitably and use simple words about a fabric

- Test fabrics simply and begin to describe their properties, e.g. 'this one's good because it's soft'

- Explore a range of fabrics and describe their properties and suitability, e.g. 'the sponge is squashy and warm and would be good for granny'

Whole class or group activity

Using the Image Bank pictures 3.4–3.7 of characters from stories, introduce each character and explain the properties of the fabrics needed, for example:

Cinderella is going to the ball and needs a sparkly dress
Humpty Dumpty has a round tummy and needs stretchy trousers
Red Riding Hood is visiting granny and needs a waterproof cloak
Granny is ill in bed and needs a squashy mattress.

Organise children so that they are testing a variety of materials to select the most appropriate for a character; the relevant Image Bank picture could now be displayed on each character's table for reference. Create templates for the characters. Show individuals, where necessary, how to test the fabrics, cut shapes and stick on the character template. Talk to them about the fabric they are testing, i.e. 'Is it the best one to use?' 'Is something else better?'

When the character templates have been finished show them to the class and talk about why they have chosen the particular fabric. If possible, dress up adults or dolls with suitable fabrics so that they, in character, can talk about how good the class selections were.

Other related activities:

Exploration: continue testing and choosing fabrics for other story characters chosen by children

Writing/drawing: getting dressed, story character or themselves

Art: continue using templates of story characters or themselves in different situations, e.g. going to a party

Resources and preparation

Image Bank pictures 3.4–3.7; collection of fabrics; scissors; pipettes; small pots of water; character templates

Role play

House containing domestic play equipment and story character clothes

29

Activity ③ What is it made of?

Purpose of activity

To introduce common materials and how they are used in everyday objects

Vocabulary

names of materials: wood, metal, plastic; names of objects: spoons, chair, etc.

Assessment

Children will be able to:

- Say what the objects are made from

- Explore objects to find out more about them

- Describe features of objects, e.g. 'it's made of wood, it's hard and smooth.'

Resources and preparation

Image Bank picture 3.8; story of *Goldilocks and the Three Bears*; labels with types of material, e.g. wood, plastic, metal; collection of objects made from different materials labelled as wood, metal, etc.

Whole class or group activity

Read the story of *Goldilocks and the Three Bears* and ask children to look closely at Image Bank picture 3.8, which shows the three bears' kitchen. Ask the children what the things in the room are made of, for example: wooden chairs, spoons, metal saucepans, china bowls. Use actual examples to help with the categorisation.

Give out a selection of labels to the children (either labels of different materials or the same) and ask them to walk around the classroom and put labels on objects they can find. Talk to them about the materials they can find, particularly combinations such as chairs with plastic and metal pieces.

Bring the class or group together again and talk about what they have found. Are some things made of different materials, e.g. spoons being plastic, wood or metal and chairs being fabric, plastic, wood or metal?

Ask children if the objects could be made of other things, e.g. 'Could a spoon be made of china?' 'Could a chair be made of glass?' To finish, ask them to look at things at home and see what they are made of, e.g. their toys.

Role play

Three bears' house: domestic play equipment of different materials but not electrical appliances.

Other related activities:

Exploration: display of labelled objects, e.g. wood and plastic spoons

Writing/drawing: a room within a story character's house, e.g. Cinderella's castle, with labels for each type of material, or room in own house

Mathematics: matching size of object to bear using drawings or objects, e.g. sizes of spoon, bowl, chair and bed

Activity ❹ Which porridge tastes the best?

Purpose of activity

To introduce how to make and taste porridge flavours

Vocabulary

porridge, oats, milk, water, salt, salty, sugar, sweet, ingredients, mix, stir, cook, heat, hot, taste, favourite

Assessment

Children will be able to:

● Say what flavour the porridge is and whether they like it or not

● Recognise the difference in flavours

● Describe the porridge flavours and talk about how they are different

Whole class or group activity

Using the *Goldilocks and the Three Bears* story again, ask children about porridge. Find out how many have eaten porridge, how many like it, how it is made.

Tell the children that they are going to see which flavour of porridge they like best, e.g. salty, sweet or plain, and use the characters in the story to help with the preferences using the Image Bank pictures 3.9–3.11.

Organise small groups of pupils to work with an adult in making porridge and flavouring it according to the character. All children can make the porridge and flavour it or not. *(For recipe see page 59.)*

Once the different porridge flavours have been cooked children and adults taste each to see which one they prefer. Once they have chosen their favourite they can write their name on a cut-out bowl and stick this to the graph in the appropriate place. A version of this graph could also be compiled using ICT.

At the end of the session, show all children the graph and ask them which flavour was the favourite of the class and which the least favourite. If possible, graphs from other classes can be compared.

Other related activities:

Cooking: continue with favourite sandwich fillings and recording the findings once more onto a class graph

Writing/drawing/ICT: make a sequence about making porridge

Resources and preparation

Image Bank pictures 3.9–3.11; porridge ingredients (*recipe p.59: oats, sugar, salt, milk, water*); saucepans and spoons; large class graph (axes: flavour of porridge/no. of children); paper bowls and plastic spoons for tasting porridge

 Make sure you have enough adult help in making porridge

 Ensure children are told about hygiene — not licking the cooking spoon, washing hands, etc.

Role play

Three bears' house:

Activity ❺ What do I like best?

Purpose of activity

To use favourite foods as a way of recording a survey

Vocabulary

favourite, like most, like least; types of food: crisps, jelly, fruit, etc.; flavour, types of flavour: sweet, sour, tangy, orangy, etc.

Assessment

Children will be able to:

● Describe the taste of food simply, e.g. 'nice', 'yuck'

● Recognise the difference in flavours, e.g. 'that's orangy', 'that's strawberry'

● Describe the flavours and talk about how they are different

Whole class or group activity

Use a particular food type to introduce how to make a class survey of favourites, e.g. crisp flavour, fruit, jelly flavour, using real examples.

Organise the activity as a circus of different foods to taste with perhaps one group of children taking food around the class for others to taste as a separate survey.

Talk to children about their preferences and why they like the tastes. Use the food shapes for children to write their name on and record on a large class or group graph. A version of the graph could also be made using ICT.

Once all the findings have been collected and a graph or number of graphs have been made, discuss the findings as a class. If possible, compare with findings from another class. Discuss questions related to which was the favourite flavour and encourage children to ask their own questions about the graphs.

Other related activities:

Mathematics: use Image Bank 3.12 as an example to discuss favourites

Writing/drawing: make a favourite food leaflet for the café

ICT: create menus for the café

Resources and preparation

Image Bank picture 3.12; disposable bowls and spoons for tasting; food types for tasting, e.g. crisps, jelly, apples, smarties, etc.

⚠ Ensure that children's allergies to foods are checked before any tasting

⚠ Ensure children wash their hands before tasting the food

Role play

Three bears could open a café

Make menus and have visitors such as parents or other staff to be served

Activity 6 Which things work by electricity?

Purpose of activity

To introduce the idea that electricity is used to make some things work
To remind children about safety issues

Vocabulary

electricity, wire, plug, names of appliances

Assessment

Children will be able to:

● Name an appliance that works by electricity

● Show an awareness of how the appliance works

● Name a variety of appliances that work by electricity

Whole class or group activity

Use the classroom to talk about the appliances in the room that use electricity to make them work. Talk about how the object is plugged in and turned on. Look at each example together and make or draw a list: computer, television, lights, etc.

Compare Image Bank picture 3.8 of the three bears' kitchen again with the modern day kitchen (3.13). Talk about the differences. Look at the picture of the modern kitchen and talk about the appliances they can see that use electricity, e.g. microwave, toaster, etc.

Give out a selection of photos of different rooms (Image Bank pictures 3.14–3.16) and ask children to talk to each other about the appliances seen. Ask them to write or draw a list of all the electrical appliances they can see.

At the end of the session show or read out the lists made.

Other related activities:

Art: cut and stick electrical appliances from magazines. Could be a collection of appliances or a comparison, e.g. works by electricity or not

Writing/drawing: electrical appliances in own bedroom showing plugs, wires and on/off button

Resources and preparation

Image Bank pictures 3.8, 3.13–3.16

⚠ Remind children about how careful we need to be with electricity, e.g. not putting fingers into a socket or using water near appliances

Role play

Three bears' house/café, modernised with appliances that would work by electricity, e.g. iron, microwave, etc.

UNIT 4 Moving Around

Unit guidance

Purpose of unit:

- To explore how people and everyday objects move by pulls

By the end of the topic children will be able to:
- Sort objects by one function
- Talk about what is seen and what is happening
- Examine objects and living things to find out more about them
- Ask questions about why things happen and how things work

Activities

1 How can I make things move?
Exploring pushes and pulls

2 How can I make toys move?
Further exploration

3 What makes objects move?
Exploring a variety of pushes and pulls

4 How can I make my friend move?
Exploring moving and not moving

5 What can I make with plasticine?
Making models

6 What can I make with playdough?
Making and cooking dough shapes

Links to other areas of learning:

PS&E: involvement; persistence; interest; initiate ideas; speak in the familiar group

CL&L: listen to stories; begin to use more complex sentences; talk alongside others; initiate conversation; link statements about a theme; speak audibly and with confidence

MD: begin to talk about shapes; use appropriate shapes; adapt shapes

K&U: construct pieces; construct with a purpose

PD: move freely; demonstrate control; different ways of moving; manipulate materials; move with confidence and control

CD: put sequence of movement together; capture experiences in paint, etc.

> ### Teaching resources
>
> Big Story Book: 'A plasticine snowman'
>
> Image Bank
>
> Display and collections: toys that move
>
> Children's artwork: plasticine models

> ### Role play examples
>
> House
>
> Toy shop or factory
>
> Garage

Activity ❶ How can I make things move?

Purpose of activity

To introduce the idea of pushes and pulls causing movement of objects

Vocabulary

push, pull, in, out, up, down, move, moving

Assessment

Children will be able to:

- Say how an object can be pushed or pulled

- Examine objects and find out how they can be pushed or pulled

- Identify movement in more complex objects, e.g. tricycle

Whole class or group activity

Show Image Bank picture 4.1 and talk about how the objects are made to move. Demonstrate for children to follow that a push or pull is done in a particular direction.

Walk around the room or show examples of objects that can be moved by a push or a pull. Describe each movement and stick a ready prepared label on the objects concerned. Demonstrate the push or pull (or both) and ask the children to repeat the words and movements.

Give out ready prepared 'push' and 'pull' labels and ask children to label objects around the room and outside, including the play equipment. When the labels have been used up ask the children to walk around the room and test the objects.

'How does it move?' 'Did you use a push or a pull?'

Talk about how things are made to move, e.g. push, pull or both.

Bring children together and record on a chart (sets or Venn diagram) some of the objects that can be made to move by a push, pull or both.

Other related activities:

Communication: using Image Bank pictures 4.2, 4.3 and 4.4, ask children, in pairs, to talk about the pushes and pulls they can see in the everyday pictures.

Physical: use of play equipment and apparatus to find out about pushes and pulls

Resources and preparation

Image Bank pictures 4.1–4.4; 'push' and 'pull' labels (three of each for each child); blutac; have available some outdoor play equipment, e.g. tricycles; Image Bank pictures 4.3, 4.12–4.16 (for role play)

Role play/small world

Garage, supermarket or toy shop/factory

Activity ❷ How can I make the toys move?

Purpose of activity

To apply the children's practical knowledge of pushes and pulls to toys

Vocabulary

push, pull, move, forwards, backwards, up, down, twist, turn, fast, slow

Assessment

Children will be able to:

● Use vocabulary to say how the toy moves

● Show an awareness of how the toy can change its movement

● Begin to ask questions about how a toy moves

Whole class or group activity

Remind children of the labelled objects in the room and show them Image Bank pictures 4.5 and 4.6 to introduce them to making toys move. Talk about the collection of toys relating them to the pictures where possible. Ask children if they can see how the toys can be made to move and ask some children to demonstrate the push, pull or both with examples from the collection.

In small groups ask children to test the movement of toys and sort them into groups of 'push' and 'pull' using sorting hoops. Ask children to draw each set and label the drawings appropriately. Extend the activity by testing toys to see whether they move more or differently if they are pulled or pushed harder or more gently.

Show children's sorting and drawings and talk about how the toys have been made to move. Finish the session, or leave to later in the day, by reading the story from Unit 2 about a toy car being pushed under the bed. Talk about how objects can be made to move fast or slow by the amount of push or pull.

Other related activities:

Exploration: continue exploring movement of toys

Physical: use wheeled vehicles outside and talk about how they can be made to move

History: talk about old and new toys/teddies, etc.

Mathematics: continue sorting 'pushes' and 'pulls'

Resources and preparation

Image Bank pictures 4.5 and 4.6; Big Story Book story 'Can you see my new toy car?'; sorting hoops; collection of toys, old and new, that can be moved by a push or a pull; Image Bank pictures 4.3, 4.12–4.16 (for role play)

Role play/small world

Garage, supermarket or toy shop/factory

Activity ❸ What makes objects move?

Purpose of activity

To consolidate children's understanding of how they can make a variety of objects move

Vocabulary

push, pull, fast, slow, up, down, forwards, backwards, twist, round

Assessment

Children will be able to:

● Talk about how the objects are made to move, e.g. 'it's going round'

● Show how objects can change their movement

● Begin to ask questions about how objects move, e.g. 'What does it do?'

Whole class or group activity

Show children how the room has been set up as a circus of different activities. Demonstrate what is in each area, e.g. a table with construction kits, floor area with a variety of balls, balloons, large play equipment and water tray of bubbles.

Ask how the objects are made to move and organise groups of pupils to move around the areas at given time intervals. Focus children's attention on how the objects move and challenge them with how they can make things move differently, e.g. make the ball bounce higher, the bubble become bigger or the tricycle go faster. If appropriate, ask children to draw a picture about making their objects move with captions written by an adult or independently.

Finish with demonstrations of each activity by children who volunteer.

Other related activities:

Discussion: use Image Bank picture 4.7 to talk about classroom activities and focus on how the objects are made to move

Art: make ball and bubble prints as a way of recording the activities

Dance: with or without music interpret movement of bubbles and balloons

Resources and preparation

Prepare a circus of activities using the tables in the classroom and equipment outside; Image Bank picture 4.7; Image Bank pictures 4.3, 4.12–4.16 (for role play)

⚠ If bubbles are used, ensure children with allergies to soapy solutions are recognised

Role play/small world

Garage, supermarket or toy shop/factory

Activity 4 How can I make my friend move?

Purpose of activity

To introduce the idea that pushes and pulls make things move and sometimes not move if the push or pull is not hard enough

Vocabulary

push, pull, move, not move, forwards, backwards, sideways, etc.

Assessment

Children will be able to:

● Talk about how their friend is moving or not

● Show how pushes and pulls can make the movement change

● Look carefully at how pushes and pulls make or don't make things move

Whole class or group activity

Use a large space in the classroom, outside, or in the hall and remind children about how they can move their hands and feet, etc., from the first unit, All About Me.

Ask children to find a friend and then watch a demonstration. Using another adult or a child volunteer, one person pushes the other to make them move, then pulls to make them move. Then demonstrate pushes and pulls which do not make the other move. Show that sometimes pushes and pulls make things move — and sometimes they don't.

Give instructions to the pairs of children, e.g. 'push your friend to make them move', 'pull your friend to make them not move', etc. Walk around as children are working together to talk about how their bodies are moving and what is making them move or not.

Use Image Bank picture 4.8 and activity experiences to act out the story of The Enormous Turnip so that the actions of pushing/pulling, moving/not moving can be felt through the story.

Other related activities:

Story: cut and stick the story of The Enormous Turnip in the right order. Draw and talk about a scene from the story

Mathematics: sort the story into things are which pushed or pulled, e.g. pulling the turnip without making it move

Drama: further acting out of the story

Resources and preparation

Image Bank picture 4.8; story of 'The Enormous Turnip'; timetable the use of the hall, or use outside or a cleared area in the classroom; Image Bank pictures 4.3, 4.12–4.16 (for role play)

Ensure children push or pull each other gently

Role play/small world

Garage, supermarket or toy shop/factory

Activity 5 What can I make with plasticine?

Purpose of activity

To relate the idea of pushing and pulling to following instructions for making a plasticine snowman and other models

Vocabulary

push, pull, round, stretch, squash, roll

Assessment

Children will be able to:

● Show curiosity when manipulating plasticine

● Examine plasticine to see how it can be modelled

● Use simple vocabulary to identify some features about the properties of plasticine

Whole class or group activity

Use the snowman instructions from the Big Story Book to read to children along with the Image Bank example (4.9) and plasticine. Read out the instructions and ensure that children are using the movements described in the text to make the snowman. They could practise the instructions as a mime before using the plasticine.

Divide the children into pairs and ask each child to practise making a simple model or shape, e.g. dog, sausage or face, ready to give instructions to their friend. Focus children's attention to the words associated with forces: push, pull, squash, stretch, roll, etc.

When they have practised making their model enough, ask them to give instructions verbally to their friend, describing how to make their model. Where appropriate some children could draw pictures and/or write the instructions for their friend. Try out the model making a few times and swap instructions amongst the group.

At the end of the session show the models that have been made and read a set of instructions and ask which of the models the instructions describe.

Other related activities:

Exploration: continue making models with plasticine, focusing on the language of how the models are being made

Art: make scenery for plasticine snowmen or other models

Discussion: using Image Bank picture 4.10, talk about how the models are made and try to copy some from the pictures

Resources and preparation

Big Story Book story 'A plasticine snowman'; Image Bank pictures 4.9 and 4.10; coloured plasticine; model-making boards; rolling pins and other plasticine tools; Image Bank pictures 4.3, 4.12–4.16 (for role play)

⚠ Ensure children with allergies to plasticine are protected or use an alternative, e.g. clay

Role play/small world

Garage, supermarket or toy shop/factory

Activity 6 What can I make with playdough?

Purpose of activity

To consolidate how some materials can be manipulated and made into models, in this case using playdough as a comparison with plasticine

Vocabulary

push, pull, twist, stretch, squash, etc.

Assessment

Children will be able to:

● Show curiosity when manipulating playdough

● Examine playdough to see how it can be modelled

● Use simple vocabulary to identify some features about the properties of playdough and how it changes when it is cooked

Whole class or group activity

Review the outcomes of the previous activity and show Image Bank picture 4.11 to illustrate the variety of models that can be made from playdough rather than plasticine. Make the playdough with the children so that they can talk about the ingredients and the changes that occur as it is made.

Provide a purpose to the model making, such as making food for the role-play area (fruit/vegetables for the supermarket; general food for a house; garage mechanics' lunch). Ensure that while children are making models they are talking about the shapes they make and how the shapes change as they are being pushed, pulled and twisted.

Collect the models and cook them so that they are hardened and talk about how they are different from the uncooked playdough. Encourage discussion about the differences. Display the models and then use them in the role-play area.

Other related activities:

Exploration: continue with other playdough models and/or look at differences between playdough and plasticine when making similar models, e.g. 'Is it better to make a cup from plasticine, uncooked or cooked playdough?'

Art: use paint to finish playdough models

Resources and preparation

Image Bank picture 4.11; classroom-made playdough (recipe p.58) or salt dough; hob for making the playdough and oven for baking the playdough models: Image Bank pictures 4.3, 4.12–4.16 (for role play)

⚠ Ensure that children with allergies to playdough are recognised and an alternative, such as clay, used instead

Role play/small world

Garage, supermarket or toy shop/factory

UNIT 5 Growing Up

Unit guidance

Purpose of unit:

- To recognise changes to humans and animals as they get older

By the end of the topic children will be able to:
- Describe simple features

- Show an awareness of change

- Look closely at similarities, differences, patterns and change

- Ask questions about themselves and animals

Activities

1 How have I changed?
   Observing changes from a baby to adult

2 Who is in my family?
   Exploring differences in clothes

3 What can we do?
   Observing babies, toddlers and children

4 What do I eat during the day?
   Discussing and classifying food

5 What can animals do?
   Observing pets

6 How do animals change?
   Recognising changes as animals grow up

Links to other areas of learning:

PS&E: increase curiosity; work together; develop a
       sense of belonging

CL&L: increase confidence in communicating
       through speech, ICT and writing

MD: use of language to describe sizes

K&U: discuss and recognise the past and future
       through changes in growing up

PD: recognise healthy practices, e.g. need
       for food

CD: observing changes through variety of media

Teaching resources

Big Story Book: 'My shoes'

Image Bank

Display and collections:
clothing and food groups

Children's artwork: food
collage and models

Role play examples

House

Vet's practice

Activity ❶ How have I changed?

Purpose of activity

To demonstrate how we all change as we get older

Vocabulary

baby, toddler, child, adult, young, old, younger, older, age

Assessment

Children will be able to:

● Show curiosity about changes to themselves

● Notice and comment on changes in photographs

● Look at and describe differences in a range of photographs

Whole class or group activity

Show the collection of photographs of the class as babies, toddlers and recently. If this is not possible use a selection of teachers' and classroom assistants' photographs.

In pairs or groups the children can talk to each other about how they have changed, using the body parts vocabulary from the All About Me unit.

Display the photographs on a table and ask the children to play a 'guess who?' game using their baby photos. Can they identify each other? Can they give reasons as to how they worked out who the person was?

Show the class photographs of your own life from baby, child, teenager and adult. Discuss the different stages. Add to a display using a 'life line' with labels showing the stage and age. Look at the changes and begin to discuss the differences. Add pupils' or others' photos under the correct stages (baby, toddler, child) on the life line.

Other related activities:

Art: cut and stick pictures of different stages of life, e.g. babies, toddlers, onto a large class collage

Writing and drawing: about themselves as babies or toddlers

Resources and preparation

Ask children to collect photos of themselves as a baby, toddler and one more recent

Own or another adult's photographs over time, with stage labelled, e.g. baby, child, teenager, etc., attached to a long piece of string to symbolise life line

Role play

House containing domestic play equipment, including writing and drawing materials

Activity **2** Who is in my family?

Purpose of activity

To use the idea of family to discuss size/type of clothes

Vocabulary

adult, child, etc., mother, father, step father, granny, etc. plus names of people

Assessment

Children will be able to:

● Talk about the characters simply

● Show an awareness of differences between character ages and sizes

● Ask questions about the fictional families

Whole class or group activity

Show Image Bank picture 5.1 with the fictional family and talk about what can be seen about the characters within the picture. Give each character a name and then ask questions, e.g. 'How old do you think … is?' 'Would … have bigger shoes than … ?' 'Is … older than … ?'

Encourage children to ask their own questions and discuss the answers together.

Once the characters have been discussed, use the collection of clothes to sort and link to one or more of the characters. Talk to the children about why they have chosen the particular set of clothes.

At the end of the session show the variety of clothes that have been selected for each character and ask children to present their ideas to each other with reasons, e.g. 'I chose these trousers for … because they will be strong for when she crawls on the floor.'

At the end of the session or later: read the Big Story Book story 'My shoes' to show how a child changes over time as an introduction to the next session.

Other related activities:

Exploration/mathematics: continue sorting type and size of clothes for other fictional families in Image Bank pictures 5.2 and 5.3 and from familiar stories

Art: group paint or collage a large picture of a family showing size

Writing/drawing/ICT: picture of own family showing different sizes

> ### Resources and preparation
>
> Image Bank picture 5.1; Big Story Book story 'My shoes'; collection of clothes suitable for the fictional family in picture 5.1

> ### Role play
>
> House containing domestic play equipment, including a variety of dolls with clothes of different sizes and uses

Activity ❸ What can we do?

Purpose of activity

To review the idea of growing up and comparing different stages

Vocabulary

newborn, baby, toddler, etc.; ages: days, months, years; activities: feed, feeding, eat, eating, sleep, sleeping, crawl, crawling

Assessment

Children will be able to:

● Talk about what is happening, e.g. 'baby talking'

● Show an awareness of change comparing babies with toddlers

● Ask questions about what babies, etc., can do

Whole class or group activity

Talk to children about a common set of questions that can be used with each child that comes in to the classroom, e.g. 'What do they eat?' 'How do they move?' 'How much do they sleep?' 'What can they do?' 'Can they walk/talk?' etc. Record these on a large class/group list for reference.

Starting preferably at newborn (ish), then 6 months, 1 year, 18 months, 2 years, etc. Observe a variety of activities, e.g. feeding, having a bath, playing, crawling, sleeping, and support children in identifying and verbalising the similarities and differences. Take photographs of each child to help with a display.

Create a display with drawings, labels, charts (e.g. times for sleeping/eating/playing) and writing about each child that is brought in.

Read the Big Story Book story 'My shoes' again and relate the size of shoe to the display, e.g. 'Which shoe would fit … ?'

Other related activities:

Writing/drawing: using their knowledge about one of the children brought in, write/draw a short biography about what the child is like and what he/she can do. Could also use own brother or sister as the subject.

ICT: use writing and drawing program to complete biography

Dance/drama: show different body movements and activities for each child's age and maturity

Exploration: which bath toys and objects float and sink? Display findings

Resources and preparation

Ask parents and carers about bringing in other children of different ages, e.g. newborn, 6 months, 1 year, 18 months, etc., which could be spread out over a number of days; Big Story Book story 'My shoes'

 Ensure children are aware of how vulnerable young babies and toddlers are

Role play

House containing domestic play equipment, including clothing and different doll sizes

Activity ❹ What do I eat during the day?

Purpose of activity

To review the times and types of food eaten during a school day

Vocabulary

food, drink, breakfast, lunch, tea, dinner, snack types of food: cereal, milk, cheese, sandwich, orange juice, ham, tomato, pizza, etc.

Assessment

Children will be able to:

● Recognise and sort a particular type of food, e.g. for breakfast

● Talk about the different sorts of food they have for lunch

● Describe the differences between the foods they have at different times of the day and ask questions about how foods can be combined

Whole class or group activity

Discuss the times within the day when they eat meals and snacks and talk about the names of these meals e.g. breakfast, lunch. Show the Image Bank pictures 5.5 and 5.6 and talk about what different children eat during the day for breakfast, lunch and dinner. Talk to the children about what they eat and notice any similarities and differences with the pictures. The class could compare actual lunch boxes or meals at lunchtime with the pictures if appropriate. Begin to categorise the types of food, e.g. types of vegetable, meat and different drinks. Record these on a large class/group chart and encourage children to find examples of each type of food in a magazine to add to the chart.

Once the chart has been completed, talk about how the foods could be combined, e.g. 'Would you have cornflakes with orange juice and not milk?' 'Would you have custard on a pizza?' Encourage children to ask their own questions.

Other related activities:

Writing/drawing/ICT: use a story character as a way of describing the sorts of food they would eat in the day: 'Would the three bears always have porridge for breakfast?'

Art: using everyday materials make and paint a plate of food for a particular meal in the day

> **Preparation and safety**
>
> Image Bank pictures 5.5 and 5.6; magazines; scissors; glue; use children's own lunch boxes, if appropriate, alongside the Image Bank

> **Role play**
>
> House containing domestic play equipment, including clothing and food

Activity **5** What can animals do?

Purpose of activity

To begin to look at animals and ask questions about them

Vocabulary

feed, feeding, eat, eating, sleep, sleeping, move, moving, etc.

Assessment

Children will be able to:
- Show curiosity about pets

- Show an awareness of a variety of pets and what they can do

- Ask questions about what pets can do

Whole class or group activity

Remind children of the criteria used when they talked about children at different stages, e.g. 'What does a baby eat?' 'How long does a toddler sleep?' Use these questions as a basis for ones to ask about pets and talk about how you can't have toddler dogs, for example.

When the pets are brought in during the day allow children to observe each one and talk about what they see as a class or a group. Use the set of questions to find out about each pet and record the answers on a large chart, one for each type of animal.

Once all the information is collected talk about the similarities and differences between each pet. For example, 'Which pets eat meat?' 'Which pets don't seem to sleep?' Encourage children to ask their own questions about the record of findings, e.g. 'Do all rabbits eat lettuce?'

Other related activities:

Observation: If possible, have a pet staying in the classroom for the day to observe and draw pictures about, e.g. fish, hamster

Art/ICT: create paintings, drawings and models of each pet

Mathematics: create a block graph of type of animal and how many children have the animal as a pet

Resources and preparation

Arrange for pets to be brought into the classroom at different times in the day or same time, depending on the type of pet; large sheets of paper to record findings about each pet; Image Bank pictures 5.7 and 5.8 (for role play)

⚠ When pets are brought in to the classroom ensure that children's allergies are known and the appropriate precautions taken, e.g. open windows, keep child away from pet, no handling, etc.

⚠ Ensure that children understand how to behave with pets

Role play

Vet's practice, including toy animals, equipment, uniforms and reception area.

Activity **6** How do animals change?

Purpose of activity

To use the idea of growing up with common animals to look at similarities and differences

Vocabulary

young, baby, adult, old; ages: days, months, years; changes related to height: tall, taller, short, shorter; and size: big, bigger, small, smaller

Assessment

Children will be able to:

- Show curiosity about changes as animals grow

- Notice and comment on changes in animals as they grow

- Look at and describe differences in a range of animals as they grow

Resources and preparation

Image Bank pictures 5.9–5.16; string; small pieces of drawing paper; blutac/sellotape; Image Bank pictures 5.7 and 5.8 (for role play)

Whole class or group activity

Use Image Bank picture 5.9 as an example of how a common animal (dog) changes as it grows from a newborn to an adult. Talk about the associated language, e.g. newborn, puppy, adult, young, old, and refer to the photographs as the discussion develops. Remind children about the pets they saw previously and ask them to talk about the dog/dogs that came into school.

Organise the children into smaller groups to study a variety of animals. For example, use information books showing life histories of particular animals with one group, CD-ROMs with another group and the Image Bank pictures 5.10–5.16 with another group. Ask children to draw the different stages in the animal's life to create a life line to display with the human life line previously made.

Discuss with the class or group what they have done and draw together the similarities and differences between the animals and how they change when they grow.

Role play

Vet's practice, including toy animals, equipment, uniforms and reception area

Other related activities:

Writing/drawing: continue other animal life lines for the display

Music: use instruments to interpret the movement of animals, e.g. playful puppy, butterfly, duckling, etc.

Dance/drama: enact the stages of growth of a frog or butterfly to music

UNIT 6 Outdoors

Unit guidance

Purpose of unit:

- To explore plants and animals found in the school grounds and other habitats

By the end of the topic children will be able to:

- Show curiosity and describe simple features
- Examine living things to find out more about them
- Look closely at similarities and differences

Activities

1 What plants can we find?
   Observing outdoor plants

2 How does a bean grow?
   Observing and sorting seeds

3 How does a sunflower grow?
   Keeping a diary about sunflowers

4 What minibeasts can we find?
   Observing minibeasts and insects

5 How do minibeasts move?
   Observing movement

6 What can we find in the pond?
   Observing animals and plants

Links to other areas of learning:

PS&E: show care for living things; motivation, concentration and interest

CL&L: communicate with increasing confidence through speech and writing

MD: talk about and use mathematical language to describe size and shape

K&U: use ICT to communicate observations; construct models and recognise 'place'

PD: use dance to interpret movement; use tools and equipment for models

CD: use music to interpret animal movements; create 2-D and 3-D pictures and models

Teaching resources

Big Story Book: 'Down by the shed'

Image Bank

Display and collections: plants and animals

Children's artwork: sunflower diary, 3-D flowers

Role play examples

Garden centre

Activity ❶ What plants can we find?

Purpose of activity

To introduce the range of outdoor plants in the school grounds or elsewhere

Vocabulary

plant, tree, flower, grass, bush, leaf, stem, trunk, outside, garden

Assessment

What children will be able to do:

● Show curiosity and describe simple features, e.g. leaf of a plant

● Examine plants to find out more about them

● Describe and identify features of plants, e.g. 'the holly leaf is shiny and prickly'

Whole class or group activity

Use the Image Bank pictures 6.1–6.4 to show children the different sorts of plants they will find, e.g. grass, trees, flowers. Using a real plant (with labels to illustrate the parts), talk about the parts of the plant, the leaf, stem and flower.

Once in the school grounds, school garden or at the favoured location, encourage children to look at the different types of plant around — trees, bushes, grass or flowers — and ensure that children recognise that they are all called plants. Ask children, in pairs, to become experts of particular parts of plants, e.g. leaves, stems and flowers, and draw the different sorts they find on a piece of paper. If it is at all possible, one leaf from each type of plant could be collected (for later sorting) or preserved (pressed and displayed between two pieces of sticky-back plastic) when children have returned to the classroom.

Return to the classroom and using the plant at the beginning of the session show how their drawings have a great variety of leaves, etc. Display children's drawings and preserved leaves in the role play garden centre.

Other related activities:

Art: large sheets of paper for drawing, cut and stick or painting different shaped leaves, stems or flowers found on their visit

Mathematics: sort the variety of leaves collected using own criteria, e.g. colour, shape and size

Preparation and safety

Prepare class or group for walking around the school grounds or for a trip to a field, garden or wood where children will be able to see a variety of plants; Image Bank pictures 6.1–6.4; label a flowering plant: leaf, stem, flower; Image Bank pictures 6.5 and 6.6 (for role play)

⚠ Ensure that children are clear about not eating any plants and washing their hands after touching them

⚠ Ensure that children are reminded about safety issues when outdoors

Role play

Garden centre with seed packets, tools, plants, plant pots, serving counter, till

Activity ❷ How does a bean grow?

Purpose of activity

To introduce a variety of seeds and observe similarities and differences

Vocabulary

seed, bean, plant, grow, water, soil; words associated with seeds: e.g. stripy, round

Assessment

Children will be able to:

● Show curiosity and describe simple features, e.g. small

● Examine seeds to find out more about them

● Describe and identify features of seeds e.g. 'it's stripy, round and pointy'

Whole class or group activity

Show Image Bank picture 6.7 and read the story *Jack and the Beanstalk*. Throw five beans out of the window or into a soil-filled tray to provide the start of a discussion about plants growing. Show Image Bank picture 6.8 to show how beans grow over time. Begin a 'bean diary' following the growth of the five beans, or other beans planted that may be more successful. Use as a class record and as a way of demonstrating to children how a diary could be kept. The demonstration will also support children's own diary of sunflowers later in the unit.

For the rest of the session make available a variety of seeds and seed packets to show how each type of plant grows over time. Encourage children to look closely at the seeds and sort them into different sets using their own criteria (size, shape, colour, stripes, etc.).

Glue the sets of seeds to pieces of paper or card, with labels to show how each seed was sorted. The sorted seeds could then be displayed within the role-play garden centre.

Other related activities:

Art: make seed packets with instructions for growing. Use in role-play garden centre. Make large paper beans and flowers to display in the garden centre

ICT: draw/paint program illustrating bean growth

Preparation and safety

Image Bank pictures 6.7 and 6.8; story of *Jack and the Beanstalk*; five beans; class diary for recording bean growth; soil-filled tray; selection of beans for sorting; paper/card; glue; Image Bank pictures 6.5 and 6.6 (for role play)

(prepare five beans to grow in a pot, just in case others don't grow)

⚠ Ensure that children realise that they should not eat any of the seeds

---

Role play

Garden centre with seed packets, tools, plants, plant pots, serving counter, till

Activity ❸ How does a sunflower grow?

Purpose of activity

To continue idea of growing plants outdoors using sunflower seeds

Vocabulary

sunflower, seed, water, soil, diary

Assessment

Children will be able to:

● Show curiosity and describe simple features, e.g. sunflower

● Show an awareness of change

● Describe and identify features of plants growing, e.g. 'it needs water and soil'

Whole class or group activity

Use Image Bank picture 6.9 to illustrate how sunflowers grow from seeds that they have already seen earlier in the unit. With about three seeds each, take the children outside to plant the seeds straight into the ground (or into small pots in the classroom depending on the time of year). Three seeds should ensure that at least one seed is successful. Talk about what is needed for the sunflower seed to grow.

As the seeds are being planted, talk about what is happening and what the seeds will grow into, relating this talk to the Image Bank picture already shown.

Back in the classroom begin each child's individual diary for charting how their sunflower is growing. Have an actual seed stuck to the first page, and ask children then to draw a picture of what they did and write a simple sentence, if possible.

Continue to ask children to add details to their diaries at regular intervals, e.g. checking the sunflowers each day and recording the sunflower growth in their diary once a week with a piece of string or drawn line. Measurements can also be recorded in centimetres, if necessary.

Other related activities:

Art: paint or use another medium, e.g. collage, to recreate planting sunflowers

Dance: simulating the sequence of planting and growing sunflowers, practising without music initially

Preparation and safety

Prepare an area of soil or large tub in the school grounds for growing sunflowers, or provide small pots and soil if necessary to grow them in the classroom; Image Bank picture 6.9; packets of sunflower seeds; white garden labels for children's names to mark where their seed is planted; another adult to help with planting

Role play

Garden centre with seed packets, tools, plants, plant pots, serving counter, till

Activity ❹ What minibeasts can we find?

Purpose of activity

To introduce the variety of minibeasts (and insects) found outdoors

Vocabulary

minibeast, insect; names: centipede, worm, spider, ant, etc.

Assessment

Children will be able to:

- Show curiosity and describe simple features e.g. long legs

- Examine minibeasts to find out more about them

- Describe and identify features of minibeasts, e.g. 'the centipede is wriggly, lots of legs' 'an ant is an insect'

Whole class or group activity

Read the Big Story Book story 'Down by the shed' as an introduction then, using Image Bank pictures 6.10–6.13, introduce children to the variety of animals that can be found in the school grounds. Use the term 'animal' but distinguish between large animals such as dogs and 'minibeasts' as the sorts of animals that will be studied.

By referring to the individual minibeast photos talk about their names and the number of their legs. Display the number of legs in groups to help classify 'insects' as those with six legs, e.g. grasshopper, ant, butterfly.

Ask children about their experiences in finding minibeasts and insects *(see page 59 for a list of minibeasts they can search for)*. Talk about how they are going to find them in the school grounds, e.g. looking under stones, logs and behind walls or small buildings and on the playground and walls. Encourage children to draw pictures of the animals they find and classify them as insects or not. Some of the minibeasts could be collected in 'hotels' so that they could be studied in the classroom.

Back in the classroom ask children to use plasticine, clay or playdough to recreate the minibeasts they have found. Show the models and drawings and classify them by the number of their legs.

Other related activities:

Exploration: observation of collected minibeasts

Discussion: Image Bank picture 6.14 showing a variety of garden minibeasts

Art: ICT, drawings, paintings or 3-D models (for garden centre)

Geography: make a class map to show where the minibeasts were found

Music: use instruments to compose a walk in a garden of minibeasts

Resources and preparation

You may need to prepare stones, logs, etc. some time before this activity to ensure that there will be minibeasts to find! Big Story Book story 'Down by the shed'; Image Bank pictures 6.10–6.14; plasticine/clay/playdough; plastic containers as 'hotels' for collecting minibeasts; wooden boards and clips for supporting children drawing outside; Image Bank pictures 6.5 and 6.6 (for role play)

Role play

Garden centre, including models and pictures of minibeasts

Activity ⑤ How do minibeasts move?

Purpose of activity

To observe how minibeasts and insects move

Vocabulary

names of minibeasts, leg, forward, backward, up, down, fast, slow, wriggle, etc.

Assessment

Children will be able to:

● Show curiosity and describe simple features, e.g. wriggle

● Examine minibeasts to find out more about how they move

● Describe and identify features of minibeasts, e.g. 'the legs go forwards and backwards'

Whole class or group activity

Remind children of the minibeasts they found and how they were grouped as insects or not. Talk about how minibeasts move, using examples collected and use Image Bank picture 6.15 to provide a reference point for the types of legs a minibeast or insect has. Talk about how the legs make the body move, and encourage 'movement' vocabulary. Demonstrate how to use a magnifying glass.

Using the collected example, organise an example on each classroom table, e.g. ants, woodlice, worms, ladybirds, spiders, and organise groups of children to become experts of each minibeast in turn.

Tell children to look closely at how the minibeast 'walks' or moves. Focus children's attention on the movement of the individual legs and ask them to draw the minibeast and if possible write a short sentence about how it moves. Use Image Bank picture 6.15 for information about the different sorts of legs. After a period of time move groups of children around the classroom or leave them free to move when they finish.

Display the drawings next to the collected minibeasts and ask children to move around the room to look at each other's drawings.

Other related activities:

Dance: interpret the movement of a variety of minibeasts with or without music

Art: continue paintings and 3-D models

Mathematics/ICT: make a block graph of number of legs and names of minibeasts

Preparation and safety

Image Bank picture 6.15; collection of minibeasts in 'hotels' for close observation; magnifiying glasses (preferably one each); drawing paper; Image Bank pictures 6.5 and 6.6 (for role play)

 Ensure children take care with the minibeasts and don't handle them

Role play

Garden centre including models and pictures of minibeasts

Activity ❻ What lives in a pond?

Purpose of activity

To observe and recognise minibeasts in a pond

Vocabulary

pond, water, names of minibeasts and plants, top, bottom, float, middle

Assessment

Children will be able to:

- Show curiosity and describe simple features, e.g. round

- Examine the pond to find out more about it

- Describe and identify features of the pond, e.g. 'water boatmen live on top of the water'

Whole class or group activity

Use Image Bank picture 6.16 to introduce a pond habitat. Talk about what can be seen in the picture such as naming the different minibeasts, e.g. frog, newt, and where they live in the water, e.g. surface, floating or at the bottom.

Use the discussion to introduce the water tray pond and talk together about the animals that live in different parts of the 'pond'. Ask children to draw a picture of the pond (side view through water tray) with a simple sentence saying what can be seen.

Display the drawings and talk about the different animals and plants found. If possible, construct a diary of observations over time and talk about any changes noticed such as frogspawn hatching.

Other related activities:

Art/ICT: paintings, collage or 3-D model of a pond habitat

Music: use instruments to interpret the movement of animals in the pond

Dance: interpret the pond habitat with or without music

Resources and preparation

Some days before the session prepare a class water tray outside as a pond, using pond water with plants and minibeasts, etc. from a garden pond; Image Bank picture 6.16; Image Bank pictures 6.5 and 6.6 (for role play)

⚠ Ensure children are aware that the pond is temporary and that all the water will be returned to the garden pond later

⚠ If frogspawn is collected make sure that a suitable environment is maintained if you wish to keep the pond while tadpoles and frogs develop

⚠ Ensure children wash their hands if they touch the pond water

Role play

Garden centre including models and pictures of minibeasts from gardens or ponds

Recipe for gingerbread

This is a very simple recipe for making gingerbread men:

Ingredients:
$\frac{1}{2}$ teaspoon ground ginger
2oz (50g) caster sugar
2oz (50g) margarine
4oz (100g) self-raising flour
warmed golden syrup
Currants

Preheat oven to 350°F, 180°C, Gas Mark 4. Cream margarine and sugar. Then mix in flour and ginger. Add enough golden syrup to make the dough stiff. Roll out the dough on a floured chopping board and cut out shapes, using the currants for eyes, buttons, etc. Place on a greased baking tray and bake for approximately 10 minutes.

Instructions for playdough (enough for 3–6 children)

Ingredients:
2 cups of flour
1 cup of salt
1 tablespoon oil
1 teaspoon cream of tartar
food colouring
water

Mix all of the ingredients together, adding water as required. Place in a saucepan over a medium heat and stir until stiff. Allow to cool, then knead. It is now ready to model with.

To harden, bake in a moderate oven until brown. Brush on condensed milk mixed with food colouring before baking for added colour.

Recipe for porridge

Ingredients:
1 cup of porridge oats
3 cups of milk
Salt
Sugar

For daddy bear and mummy bear use 1 cup of porridge oats and 3 cups of milk. Bring to the boil and simmer and stir for 5 minutes, adding salt for daddy bear during cooking. For baby bear use $1/2$ cup of porridge oats and $1^1/_2$ cups of milk. Bring to the boil and simmer and stir for 5 minutes, adding some sugar during cooking.

Minibeast checklist

This checklist is to help in finding insects and other small creatures. The minibeasts on the list range from the no-legged to the many-legged. Those minibeasts with six legs are classified as insects and are marked with an (i).

Ant (i)	Mite
Aphid (i)	Moth (i)
Bee (i)	Silverfish (i)
Beetle (i)	Slug
Bumble Bee (i)	Snail
Butterfly (i)	Spider
Caterpillar (butterfly larva)	Wasp (i)
Centipede (i)	Woodlouse
Cockroach (i)	Worm
Crane fly (Daddy-long-legs) (i)	
Cricket (i)	*On/in/or around water*
Dragonfly (i)	Dragonfly (i)
Earwig (i)	Mayfly (i)
Fly (i)	Mosquito (i)
Grasshopper (i)	Pond skater (i)
Ladybird (i)	Tadpole
Millipede	Water Boatman (i)